Walking in Faith
Trusting God Every Step of the Way
Charles E. Cravey

In His Steps Publishing Company

Unless otherwise noted, all scripture is from the King James Version of the Holy Bible.

ISBN: 978-1-58535-096-4 (Paperback)

ISBN: 978-1-58535-097-1 (Kindle)

Library of Congress Catalog Number: 2025915453

Printed in the United States of America.

Published by In His Steps Publishing, Statesboro, Georgia.

Contents

Preface

Faith is not a straight line—it's a winding path, often marked by questions, quiet courage, and unexpected grace. This book was born from my own journey of walking with God through seasons of clarity and seasons of fog. It is not a manual, but a companion. Not a lecture, but a lantern.

Each chapter in *Walking in Faith* is a step—an invitation to trust, to listen, to forgive, to serve, and to hope. It is my prayer that these reflections, scriptures, and sonnets will meet you where you are and gently guide you forward.

You may be walking through a valley, standing at a crossroads, or simply longing for deeper communion with God. Wherever you find yourself, know this: you are not alone. The Shepherd walks beside you. His voice still calls. His promises still hold.

This book is for the weary and the wondering. For those who have walked long and those just beginning. May it be a gentle reminder that faith is not about perfection—it's about presence. And every step taken in trust is a step toward home.

With gratitude and grace,

Charles E. Cravey

Chapter 1

Faith That Waits in the Silence

"I wait for the Lord, my whole being waits, and in His word
I put my hope."
—Psalm 130:5 (NIV)

Opening Reflection

There are seasons when the heavens feel quiet, and our prayers
seem to echo into stillness. Yet silence is not absence—it is often

the sacred space where faith deepens. Like seeds beneath winter soil, trust grows unseen.

Scripture Meditation

- *Isaiah 30:15* — "In quietness and trust is your strength."

- *Lamentations 3:26* — "It is good to wait quietly for the salvation of the Lord."

Devotional Insight

Waiting is not wasted time. It is the posture of surrender, the soil of transformation. In the hush of unanswered prayers, God is shaping our hearts to receive more than we imagined. Faith that waits is faith that believes God is working—even when we cannot see.

Jesus Himself waited—thirty years before His public ministry began. His waiting was holy. So is ours.

Prayer Prompt

Lord, teach me to wait with hope, not despair. Help me trust Your timing, even when I long for answers. Let my silence be filled with Your presence. Amen.

Walking It Out

Today, resist the urge to rush. Sit quietly with God for five minutes. Write down what you're waiting for—and ask Him to meet you in the stillness.

The First Step of Faith

Charles E. Cravey

Upon the hush of dawn, He spoke my name.

Not with a map but promise in His hand.

No charted course, no glory, wealth, or fame—

Just trust to walk across uncharted land.

The path was veiled in morning's golden mist.

Yet still I rose, though fear clung to my side.

His voice, a compass I could not resist,

Led me through valleys deep and mountains wide.

Each step became a prayer, a sacred vow,

To follow Him where grace and mercy lead.

Though questions bloom like thorns upon the bough,

His love remains my light, my daily need.

So here I walk, not knowing all ahead—

But faith has feet, and I am Spirit-led.

Chapter 2

Steps of Surrender

Anchor Scripture

"Trust in the Lord with all your heart and lean not on your own understanding; in all your ways submit to Him, and He will make your paths straight."

—Proverbs 3:5–6 (NIV)

Opening Reflection

Surrender is not weakness—it is wisdom. It is the moment we release our grip on control and place our lives into the hands of the One who sees the whole path. Faith begins with a step, but it deepens when we let go.

Scripture Meditation

- *Luke 22:42* — "Not my will, but Yours be done."

- *Psalm 37:5* — "Commit your way to the Lord; trust in Him, and He will do this."

Devotional Insight

To surrender is to trust that God's plan is better than ours. It's the quiet courage to say yes to His leading, even when it disrupts our comfort. Jesus surrendered in Gethsemane—and through that surrender, salvation came.

When we release our need to understand, we make room for peace. Surrender is not the end of strength—it's the beginning of grace.

Prayer Prompt

Father, help me to let go of what I cannot control. Teach me to trust Your heart when I cannot trace Your hand. I surrender my plans to You. Amen.

Walking It Out

Write down one area where you're struggling to surrender. Pray over it daily this week, asking God to help you release it into His care.

The Yielded Heart

Charles E. Cravey

I held the reins with trembling, stubborn hands,
Afraid to trust what I could not foresee.
Yet grace kept calling through life's shifting sands—
"Come walk with Me, and I will set you free."

The path of peace begins where pride lets go,
Where fear dissolves beneath love's steady gaze.
Though storms may rise and winds of trial blow,
His mercy anchors me through all my days.

To yield is not to lose, but to be found—
To lay down self and rise in holy light.
In surrender, sacred truths abound,
And burdens lift beneath His wings of might.

So here I stand, arms open to the skies—
A soul released, where deeper faith shall rise.

Chapter 3

Faith in the Fog

Anchor Scripture

"For we walk by faith, not by sight."
—2 Corinthians 5:7 (NKJV)

Opening Reflection

There are days when clarity escapes us—when the road ahead is shrouded in mist and the familiar landmarks disappear. In those moments, faith becomes our compass. It's not the absence of uncertainty, but the presence of trust that keeps us moving forward.

Scripture Meditation

- *Isaiah 42:16* — "I will lead the blind by ways they have not known... I will turn the darkness into light before them."

- *Hebrews 11:1* — "Faith is confidence in what we hope for and assurance about what we do not see."

Devotional Insight

Faith in the fog is not blind—it's anchored. It holds fast to the character of God when circumstances blur. The fog may obscure the path, but it cannot hide the One who walks beside us. Like the disciples in the storm, we learn to trust not the visibility, but the voice that says, "It is I. Do not be afraid."

When we walk by faith, we learn to listen more than look.

Prayer Prompt

Lord, when the way is unclear, help me trust Your presence. Teach me to walk by faith, not by sight, and to rest in Your guiding hand. Amen.

Walking It Out

Take a walk today—literally or figuratively—and reflect on an area of your life that feels uncertain. Invite God to walk with you in that fog, and journal what you sense Him saying.

When Vision Fails, Faith Rises

Charles E. Cravey

The morning mist obscures the winding trail.

And all I see are shadows, soft and gray.

Yet still I walk, though sight and sense may fail—

For faith, not vision, lights my feet today.

The trees are veiled, the hills no longer clear,

But in the hush, I hear His whisper near.

No map is drawn, no signposts do appear,

Yet peace descends and quiets every fear.

For fog may fall, but never hides His face,

And silence speaks when hearts are tuned to hear.

Each step I take is held in love's embrace,

Each breath a prayer, each moment drawing near.

So let the mist remain—I shall not stray.

My Guide is sure. He walks with me each day.

Chapter 4

Anchored in His Promise

Anchor Scripture

"Yet he did not waver through unbelief regarding the promise of God but was strengthened in his faith and gave glory to God."
—Romans 4:20 (NIV)

Opening Reflection

Promises are easy to believe when life is smooth. But when the winds rise and the waves threaten, we discover what truly anchors us. Abraham held fast to God's word, even when the evidence seemed to contradict it. His faith was not in circumstance—but in character.

Scripture Meditation

- *Hebrews 10:23* — "Let us hold unswervingly to the hope we profess, for He who promised is faithful."

- *Numbers 23:19* — "God is not human, that He should lie... Does He promise and not fulfill?"

Devotional Insight

God's promises are not fragile—they are forged in eternity. When we anchor our faith in His word, we are tethered to truth that cannot be shaken. Abraham waited decades for Isaac, yet he never let go of hope. That kind of faith is not passive—it's persistent.

To walk in faith is to walk with expectation, even when the fulfillment is still unseen.

Prayer Prompt

Lord, help me to cling to Your promises when doubt creeps in. Strengthen my heart to believe that what You've spoken, You will bring to pass. Amen.

Walking It Out

Write down a promise from Scripture that speaks to your current season. Place it somewhere visible this week—on your mirror, dashboard, or journal—and let it anchor your thoughts.

The Anchor of His Word

Charles E. Cravey

The winds may howl, the tide may rise and roar,
Yet still I stand, unmoved upon this shore.
For though the skies grow dark and doubts appear,
His voice remains—the promise drawing near.

No storm can shake what heaven has decreed.
No wave erases what grace has guaranteed.
Though time may stretch and silence fill the air,
His word endures; His covenant is there.

I do not trust in signs or fleeting light.
But in the One whose faithfulness is sure.
His vow is strong, His mercy ever right—
A hope that holds, a truth that shall endure.

So let the tempest rage—I shall not flee.
His promise is the anchor holding me.

Chapter 5

When the Path Grows Dim

Anchor Scripture

"Even though I walk through the darkest valley, I will fear no evil, for You are with me; Your rod and Your staff, they comfort me."
—Psalm 23:4 (NIV)

Opening Reflection

There are moments in every journey when the light fades and shadows stretch long. The path ahead becomes uncertain, and fear whispers its lies. But faith is not the absence of darkness—it is the presence of God within it. When the path grows dim, His nearness becomes our light.

Scripture Meditation

- *Isaiah 43:2* — "When you walk through the fire, you will not be burned... For I am with you."

- *John 8:12* — "I am the light of the world. Whoever follows Me will never walk in darkness."

Devotional Insight

David didn't say *if* he walked through the valley—he said *when*. Darkness is part of the journey, but it is never the destination.

God walks with us through every shadow, every sorrow, every silence. His rod defends, His staff guides. We are never alone.

Faith in the dark is faith refined. It teaches us to listen, to lean, and to look for light not with our eyes but with our hearts.

Prayer Prompt

Lord, when the way is shadowed and fear surrounds me, be my light. Help me trust Your presence even when I cannot feel it. Lead me through the valley with courage and peace. Amen.

Walking It Out

Light a candle today and sit quietly with God. Reflect on a time when He walked with you through a dark season. Write a short prayer of gratitude for His presence.

Light in the Valley

Charles E. Cravey

The path grew dim, the stars refused to shine,
And silence wrapped the hills in solemn gray.
Yet still I walked, though fear crept close behind,
For faith recalled what night could not betray.

His whisper stirred the stillness of my soul.
A gentle staff that guided every stride.
Though shadows stretched and threatened to control,
His light within refused to run or hide.

The valley deep became a sacred place,
Where mercy met me in the midnight hour.
No evil dared to steal His steady grace,
No darkness dimmed His everlasting power.

So let the night descend—I shall not flee.
The Shepherd walks this path ahead of me.

Chapter 6

Faith That Waits in the Silence

Anchor Scripture

"I wait for the Lord, my whole being waits, and in His word I put my hope."
—Psalm 130:5 (NIV)

Opening Reflection

Silence can feel like absence. When prayers go unanswered and heaven seems still, we wonder if God has turned away. But silence is often the sacred space where faith matures. It is the soil where trust takes root, unseen but growing.

Scripture Meditation

- *Lamentations 3:26* — "It is good to wait quietly for the salvation of the Lord."

- *Isaiah 30:15* — "In quietness and trust is your strength."

Devotional Insight

Faith that waits is faith that listens. It does not demand answers—it leans into presence. Jesus waited in silence before the cross. Elijah heard God not in the wind or fire, but in a whisper. Silence is not punishment—it is invitation.

To wait is to believe that God is working, even when we cannot see or hear. It is the quiet courage to remain, to trust, to hope.

Prayer Prompt

Lord, teach me to wait with grace. Help me trust Your timing and rest in Your presence, even when the answers are delayed. Let my silence be filled with Your peace. Amen.

Walking It Out

Spend ten minutes in silence today. No music, no distractions. Just sit with God. Let your heart speak without words and listen for His whisper.

The Stillness Between the Prayers

Charles E. Cravey

The silence stretched like dusk across my soul.

No thunder spoke; no wind began to sing.

Yet in the hush, I found a deeper goal—

To wait and trust the shadow of His wing.

No answer came, no sign lit up the skies,

But peace began to bloom where fear had grown.

The quiet taught my heart to recognize

That faith is strongest when it stands alone.

He does not rush nor bend to mortal time.

His wisdom weaves through stillness, slow and true.

And in the pause, His presence feels sublime—

A sacred hush where hope is born anew.

So let me wait, not with despair or dread,

But with a heart that knows His word is bread.

Chapter 7

The Detours of Grace

Anchor Scripture

"You intended to harm me, but God intended it for good
to accomplish what is now being done, the saving of many
lives."
—Genesis 50:20 (NIV)

Opening Reflection

We often see detours as delays—interruptions to our plans. But God sees them as divine rerouting. Joseph's journey to Egypt was paved with betrayal, injustice, and waiting. Yet every twist was part of a greater story. Grace doesn't always take the shortest path—it takes the most redemptive one.

Scripture Meditation

- *Proverbs 16:9* — "In their hearts humans plan their course, but the Lord establishes their steps."

- *Romans 8:28* — "And we know that in all things God works for the good of those who love Him."

Devotional Insight

Detours teach us to trust the Driver. When life veers off course, faith reminds us that God is still in control. His grace meets us in the unexpected, the painful, and the confusing—and transforms it into purpose. Joseph didn't just survive the detour—he became a vessel of salvation because of it.

Sometimes the road we resist is the one that leads to healing.

Prayer Prompt

Father, help me to trust Your redirection. When life takes unexpected turns, remind me that Your grace is guiding me. Use every detour for Your glory. Amen.

Walking It Out

Reflect on a time when a setback led to unexpected growth or blessing. Write a short testimony of how God used that detour to shape your faith.

Grace in the Winding Road

Charles E. Cravey

I planned a path, straight, simple, swift, and wide,
But life bent low and turned me from my way.
The road grew rough, with sorrow as my guide.
Yet grace appeared where shadows dared to stay.

Each twist became a thread in mercy's weave.
Each pause a place where deeper truths took root.
Though dreams fell down like autumn's fragile leaves,
New life arose from disappointment's fruit.

The detour was not punishment, but plan—
A holy curve that led me to His heart.
What once felt lost was held within His span,
And broken roads became a work of art.

So let me walk where grace has drawn the line—
Each step a story shaped by love divine.

Chapter 8

Healing Along the Way

Anchor Scripture

"He said to her, 'Daughter, your faith has healed you. Go in peace and be freed from your suffering.'"
—Mark 5:34 (NIV)

Opening Reflection

Healing is not always instant. Sometimes it unfolds slowly, step by step, as we walk with God. The woman who touched Jesus' cloak didn't wait for permission—she reached out in faith. And in that moment, healing met her on the road.

Scripture Meditation

- *Psalm 147:3* — "He heals the brokenhearted and binds up their wounds."

- *Jeremiah 30:17* — "But I will restore you to health and heal your wounds," declares the Lord.

Devotional Insight

Faith is not just for the mountaintop—it's for the moments when we're limping, longing, and reaching. Healing often comes in layers: emotional, spiritual, and physical. And it rarely follows our timeline. But God is gentle with our wounds. He walks with us, tending to the broken places as we go.

Sometimes the journey itself is the healing.

Prayer Prompt

Lord, I bring You my wounds—seen and unseen. Heal me in Your time and Your way. Help me trust that You are restoring me, even when I don't feel whole. Amen.

Walking It Out

Write a letter to God about an area where you need healing. Don't filter it—be honest. Then write a second letter imagining His response to you, full of grace and compassion.

The Touch That Mends

Charles E. Cravey

I reached for Him with trembling, quiet plea.
A whisper lost amid the pressing crowd.
No strength remained, no hope to set me free—
Just faith, a thread beneath despair's dark shroud.

And in that touch, the healing light broke through.
Not loud or grand, but gentle as the rain.
His eyes met mine, and suddenly I knew
That love had found me in my silent pain.

He did not scold nor ask me to explain,
But called me "daughter," whole and truly seen.
The years of ache dissolved like morning's stain,
And peace arose where sorrow once had been.

So now I walk, restored in heart and soul—
Each step a hymn of mercy making whole.

Chapter 9

Listening for Footsteps

Anchor Scripture

"My sheep listen to My voice; I know them, and they follow Me."
—John 10:27 (NIV)

Opening Reflection

Faith is not just movement—it's response. The Shepherd walks ahead, and we follow not by sight, but by sound. His voice is gentle, steady, and unmistakable to those who know Him. In a world full of noise, listening becomes a sacred act of trust.

Scripture Meditation

- *1 Kings 19:12* — "After the fire came a gentle whisper."

- *Isaiah 30:21* — "Whether you turn to the right or to the left, your ears will hear a voice behind you, saying, 'This is the way; walk in it.'"

Devotional Insight

God doesn't shout over the chaos—He whispers through it. To hear Him, we must quiet our hearts and lean in. Listening is not passive; it's active faith. It's the posture of a disciple, ready to move when the Master speaks.

Sometimes the most powerful step of faith is the one taken after stillness.

Prayer Prompt

Lord, tune my ears to Your voice. Help me recognize Your whisper amid the noise. Teach me to follow with confidence, knowing You go before me. Amen.

Walking It Out

Spend time in quiet today. Ask God to speak. Write down anything that stirs in your spirit—words, impressions, scriptures. Then reflect: What step might He be inviting you to take?

The Whisper That Leads

Charles E. Cravey

I strained to hear amid the clamor loud,
The world's demands, a storm without reprieve.
Yet in the hush, beyond the pressing crowd,
A whisper came that taught my soul to breathe.

No trumpet blast, no thunderous decree,
Just quiet truth that stirred my heart to move.
His voice, like wind through branches of a tree,
Spoke peace and purpose, gentle, firm, and true.

I followed not by sight, but by the sound—
Each step a trust, each pause a sacred cue.
Though paths were veiled and questions still abound,
His presence marked the way I never knew.

So let me walk where holy echoes fall,
And listen close to hear His tender call.

Chapter 10

The Courage to Forgive

Anchor Scripture

"For if you forgive other people when they sin against you, your heavenly Father will also forgive you."
—Matthew 6:14 (NIV)

Opening Reflection

Forgiveness is not forgetting—it's releasing. It's choosing grace over bitterness, even when the wound still aches. Jesus forgave from the cross, not because it was easy, but because it was necessary. Forgiveness is not weakness—it's holy strength.

Scripture Meditation

- *Colossians 3:13* — "Forgive as the Lord forgave you."

- *Luke 6:37* — "Forgive, and you will be forgiven."

Devotional Insight

To forgive is to walk in the footsteps of Christ. It is a decision that often precedes emotion—a step of obedience that leads to healing. Forgiveness doesn't excuse the wrong; it entrusts justice to God. It frees us from the prison of resentment and opens the door to peace.

Faith forgives not because it forgets but because it remembers grace.

Prayer Prompt

Lord, give me the courage to forgive. Help me release the hurt I've held and trust You with the outcome. Let Your mercy flow through me, even when it's hard. Amen.

Walking It Out

Write the name of someone you need to forgive. Pray for them—not with bitterness, but with hope. Ask God to soften your heart and begin the healing process.

The Grace to Let Go

Charles E. Cravey

The wound was deep, the silence sharp and long.
A shadow cast across my tender soul.
I held the hurt like proof of every wrong,
Afraid that grace would make the broken whole.

But mercy whispered through the bitter haze,
"Forgive, and you shall find your heart restored."
Not to forget, but choose a higher praise—
To trust the One who justice will afford.

Forgiveness is a key, not just a balm.
It frees the captive—both the wronged and wrong.
It does not rush but moves with sacred calm.
A quiet strength where healing sings its song.

So here I stand, with open hands and heart—
The grace to let go is faith's truest art.

Chapter 11

Serving With Open Hands

Anchor Scripture

"Serve one another humbly in love."

—Galatians 5:13 (NIV)

Opening Reflection

Faith doesn't just walk—it gives. It bends low, opens hands, and pours out love. Jesus washed feet, fed crowds, and healed the broken—not for applause, but for compassion. To serve is to reflect the heart of Christ, who came not to be served, but to serve.

Scripture Meditation

- *Mark 10:45* — "For even the Son of Man did not come to be served, but to serve..."

- *1 Peter 4:10* — "Each of you should use whatever gift you have received to serve others..."

Devotional Insight

Service is not a task—it's a posture. It begins with availability, not ability. When we serve with open hands, we offer not just our time but our hearts. Faith that serves is faith that sees others as sacred. It listens, lifts, and loves without condition.

The hands of faith are never empty—they are always ready.

Prayer Prompt

Lord, make me a servant. Help me to see the needs around me and respond with joy. Let my hands be open, my heart be willing, and my life reflect Your love. Amen.

Walking It Out

Find one small way to serve someone today—without being asked. Whether it's a kind word, a helping hand, or a quiet act of generosity, let it be done in love.

The Hands That Give

Charles E. Cravey

He knelt to wash the dust from weary feet.
No throne, no crown, just towel and basin near.
His hands, once raised to calm the storm's defeat,
Now served in silence, drawing others near.

No task too small, no soul too low to lift.
His love poured out in every humble deed.
Each act of grace a sacrificial gift,
A holy touch to meet the deepest need.

So let my hands reflect that sacred way,
Not clenched in pride, but open, kind, and true.
To serve is not to lose, but to obey—
To mirror Christ in all I say and do.

For faith that walks must also stoop and give.
And in that giving, learn what it means to live.

Chapter 12

The Weight of Kindness

Anchor Scripture

"He has shown you, O mortal, what is good. And what does the Lord require of you? To act justly and to love mercy and to walk humbly with your God."
—Micah 6:8 (NIV)

Opening Reflection

Kindness is not light—it carries weight. It bears burdens, lifts spirits, and heals wounds. In a world quick to judge and slow to listen, kindness becomes a radical act of faith. It is the language of heaven spoken through human hands.

Scripture Meditation

- *Ephesians 4:32* — "Be kind and compassionate to one another..."

- *Proverbs 11:17* — "Those who are kind benefit themselves, but the cruel bring ruin on themselves."

Devotional Insight

Kindness is not weakness—it is strength under control. It chooses gentleness when harshness would be easier. Jesus showed kindness to the outcast, the sinner, and the broken. His kindness restored dignity and revealed divinity.

To walk in faith is to walk in kindness—because every soul we meet is one God loves.

Prayer Prompt

Lord, make me kind. Not just in words, but in action. Help me see others through Your eyes and respond with grace, compassion, and humility. Amen.

Walking It Out

Do one intentional act of kindness today—especially for someone who may not expect it. Let it be a reflection of God's heart through yours.

The Gentle Strength of Grace

Charles E. Cravey

Kindness is weighty, though it moves with grace.
A quiet force that lifts the fallen soul.
It meets the wound, the worry, and the face
Of those who long to feel again made whole.

It does not shout nor seek the grand acclaim,
But stoops to serve where others turn away.
Its strength is found in love, not pride or fame.
Its power shown in mercy's gentle sway.

The Savior walked with kindness in His stride.
Each touch a balm, each word a healing stream.
He saw the heart that others would deride,
And gave the outcast back their hope and dream.

So let me walk with kindness as my creed—
A faith that loves and meets the deepest need.

Chapter 13

Hope on the Horizon

Anchor Scripture

"But those who hope in the Lord will renew their strength. They will soar on wings like eagles; they will run and not grow weary, they will walk and not be faint."
—Isaiah 40:31 (NIV)

Opening Reflection

Hope is the sunrise after a long night. It lifts our eyes beyond the present pain and reminds us that God is still writing the story. When our strength fades and the road stretches far, hope whispers, "Keep walking—He's not finished yet."

Scripture Meditation

- *Romans 15:13* — "May the God of hope fill you with all joy and peace as you trust in Him..."

- *Hebrews 6:19* — "We have this hope as an anchor for the soul, firm and secure."

Devotional Insight

Hope is not wishful thinking—it's confident expectation. It's rooted in the character of God, not the condition of our circumstances. When we walk in faith, hope becomes our horizon—always ahead, always drawing us forward.

Even in the waiting, even in the weariness, hope renews. It reminds us that the best is yet to come.

Prayer Prompt

Lord, fill me with Your hope. When I feel tired or discouraged, I lift my eyes to see Your promises. Help me walk with renewed strength and joyful expectation. Amen.

Walking It Out

Write down one promise of God that gives you hope. Reflect on how it has sustained you in difficult seasons. Share it with someone who may need encouragement today.

The Light Beyond the Hill

Charles E. Cravey

The road grew long, my steps began to slow,
The sky turned gray, and silence filled the air.
Yet still I walked, though weariness did grow,
For hope arose and met me in despair.

It did not shout but shimmered on the breeze.
A golden thread that tugged my heart ahead.
It whispered peace among the barren trees,
And sang of life where once I feared the dead.

The hill I climbed revealed a brighter view.
A glimpse of grace beyond the present strain.
And in that light, my strength was born anew—
A joy that danced despite the ache and rain.

So let me walk with hope as morning's song,
A faith that knows the wait will not be long.

Chapter 14

Faith That Leaves Footprints

Anchor Scripture

"I have fought the good fight, I have finished the race, I have kept the faith."

—2 Timothy 4:7 (NIV)

Opening Reflection

Faith is not just personal—it's generational. Every step we take in obedience leaves a trail for others to follow. Paul's words near the end of his life weren't about accomplishments—they were about endurance. He walked faithfully, and his footprints still guide us today.

Scripture Meditation

- *Psalm 78:4* — "We will tell the next generation the praiseworthy deeds of the Lord..."

- *Hebrews 13:7* — "Consider the outcome of their way of life and imitate their faith."

Devotional Insight

Legacy is built one step at a time. It's not about perfection—it's about persistence. When we walk in faith, we leave behind more than memories—we leave markers of grace. Our children, our communities, and even strangers may one day walk the paths we've cleared.

Faith that endures becomes a map for those who come after.

Prayer Prompt

Lord, let my life leave footprints of faith. Help me walk in a way that honors You and inspires others. May my journey point to Your goodness and grace. Amen.

Walking It Out

Think of someone whose faith has impacted your life. Write them a note of gratitude—or, if they've passed, write a prayer of thanks for their legacy. Then ask God to help you become that kind of influence for someone else.

The Trail Behind My Steps

Charles E. Cravey

I walked through storms, through silence, through the flame,
Not always sure, but always held by grace.
Each step I took was marked not by acclaim,
But by a love that lit the darkest place.

The path behind is scattered with my prayers,
With moments where I stumbled, rose, and grew.
Yet in those prints, a witness still declares
That God was faithful, kind, and always true.

I do not seek a monument or praise.
But I hope my walk will guide another soul.
That in my trail, they'll find the ancient ways,
And hear the Shepherd calling them to whole.

So let me walk with purpose, heart, and light—
A legacy of faith that shines through night.

Chapter 15

Homeward Bound

Anchor Scripture

"He will wipe every tear from their eyes. There will be no more death or mourning or crying or pain..."
—Revelation 21:4 (NIV)

Opening Reflection

Every journey has a destination. For the believer, it is not a place—it is a Person. Heaven is not just the end of suffering; it is the beginning of perfect communion. We walk in faith not just to endure but to arrive. And when we do, we will be home.

Scripture Meditation

- *John 14:2–3* — "I go to prepare a place for you... that where I am, you may be also."

- *Philippians 3:20* — "Our citizenship is in heaven..."

Devotional Insight

Faith walks forward with eternity in view. It does not cling to this world but longs for the one to come. The road may be hard, but the destination is glorious. One day, we will see Him face-to-face. Every tear will be wiped away. Every burden lifted. Every longing fulfilled.

Until then, we walk with hope—and with hearts turned homeward.

Prayer Prompt

Lord, thank You for the promise of heaven. Help me live each day with eternity in mind. Let my journey reflect Your glory, and my heart remain anchored in the hope of home. Amen.

Walking It Out

Take a moment to reflect on what "home" means to you spiritually. Write a short prayer or poem expressing your longing for heaven and your gratitude for the journey.

The Journey's End Is Grace

Charles E. Cravey

The road was long, with valleys deep and wide,
With mountain peaks and nights of aching prayer.
Yet through it all, He walked close by my side,
And whispered hope into the heavy air.

Now on the hill, I see the gates ahead.
Not wrought with gold, but love's eternal flame.
No more the tears, the fears, the words unsaid—
Just joy, and rest, and calling by my name.

The journey ends where glory meets the soul.
Where faith gives way to sight, and time to peace.
Where broken hearts are finally made whole,
And all our striving finds its sweet release.

So let me walk with heaven in my gaze—
Each step a hymn, each breath a song of praise.

Chapter 16

Closing Benediction

Closing Benediction

May you walk in faith, not by sight—

with steps steady and soul surrendered.

May the fog never frighten you,

nor the silence make you doubt His nearness.

May detours become divine appointments,

and valleys become sacred ground.

May your hands remain open,

your heart remain kind,

and your legacy be marked by mercy.

May you forgive freely, serve humbly,

and listen for the whisper of the Shepherd
who walks beside you always.

And when the road grows long,
may hope rise like the morning sun—
reminding you that every step
is leading you home.

Go now, beloved,

in the peace of Christ,

the strength of the Spirit,

and the love of the Father.

Amen.

OTHER BOOKS BY DR. CRAVEY MAY BE

PURCHASED AT:

https://drcharlescravey.com or Amazon.com/Charles Cravey

Books